Body Language

The Ultimate Guide to Mastering Body Language and Nonverbal Communication to Connect, Win and Influence People

(How to Read People's Mind, Body Language Secrets, Mind Power)

by James Clark

Table of Contents

Table of Contents

Introduction

Chapter 1 – Effective Communication

Chapter 2 – What Did You Say?

Chapter 3 – Look Me in the Eye (or Don't)

Chapter 4 – Head and Shoulders, Knees and Toes, and …

Chapter 5 – Putting it All Together

Disclaimer

While all attempts have been made to verify the information provided in this book, the author does not assume any responsibility for errors, omissions, or contrary interpretations of the subject matter contained within. The information provided in this book is for educational and entertainment purposes only. The reader is responsible for his or her own actions and the author does not accept any responsibilities for any liabilities or damages, real or perceived, resulting from the use of this information.

Introduction

Body Language, What is it and why Do I need to Know about it?

"Body language" or nonverbal communication is the conscious or sometimes unconscious way living beings communicate with one another through gestures, mannerisms, movements, facial expressions, postures, and the like. Some of the cues are overt, others are minute, but all give those who notice them an insight into what the speaker truly means.

> *The most important thing in communication is hearing what isn't said*

~ Peter F. Drucker

We humans are not the only animals to use nonverbal communication. All animals, whether we walk on two legs, four legs, or no legs at all, make themselves look "bigger" to show dominance, threat, or leadership.

For example, birds stretch out their wings and puff out their chest, bear and primates raise their arms or fore legs and stretch them wide, snakes, frogs, and other amphibious creatures inflate their throat, chest, and eyes, and almost all animals stand as tall as possible and hold their head high when attempting to show dominance or power.

Conversely, when we feel threatened or want to show submission, we "close up" or become visually smaller. Crossed body postures such as folding the arms over the chest or covering the neck with one's hand are protective stances, while keeping the head down and eyes averted indicates disinterest, dismissal, or creates distance.

There are also "micro expressions" that are so brief they can be missed altogether by someone who isn't aware of them or is not paying adequate attention in a conversation or face to face encounter.

Just as a linguist spends years becoming an expert in a spoken language, one can spend a lifetime studying body language in order to become proficient. Still, everyone can and should become a student of communication.

So, if you are ready to learn more about body language and willing to put in the effort necessary to become a student of people, let's get started.

Chapter 1 – Effective Communication

When we are born, we are already well on our way to mastering nonverbal communication. Babies cry, scream, whimper, and coo and the adults who love and care for them respond. The response is the teacher as the child grows and learns which sound to make to get the response they need.

It is this innate survival instinct among all living beings that begins our lifelong lesson in communication. Somewhere along the way however, we humans tend to stop learning how to communicate effectively, believing that if we "use our words" we will get our message delivered in the right way to the right person.

Unfortunately, there are many parts to the effective exchange of information and ideas and we would do well to learn more about them.

Communication is not just talking. The word "communication" is derived from an old Latin word "communicare" which means, "to share". When communication is successful both parties understand the information that was shared or divided between the two.

Communication always needs a giver <u>and</u> a receiver, and if those two parties involved in the discourse do not reach an understanding (this is different than agreement, although an agreement can be an understanding) then they did NOT communicate, they were just participants in a discourse.

Effective communication consists of several parts: a sender, a receiver, a message, the medium by which the message is delivered (such as spoken word, body language, written word), decoding of message by all parties, feedback, and the "static" or things that interfere with the effective delivery of the message.

The sender is the person who is trying to communicate a message, share information, or persuade another person or persons. The receiver is the person or group for whom the message or information is intended.

The message, an oft overlooked and under considered part of communication is vitally important. I'm sure you have had a conversation with someone at one time or another who didn't seem to have a clue what they were trying to say.

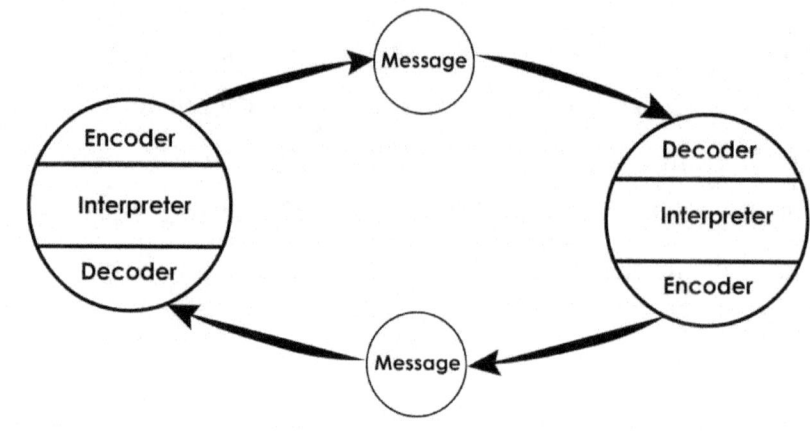

Perhaps they "talked in circles", they raised their voice or spoke too softly, or they overused place holders such as "um", "ah", or "ya know", and to further complicate your understanding, they fidgeted while speaking, paced, wrung their hands, or adjusted their clothing.

When a speaker is certain of what they want to express, what information they want to share, or what emotion they want to convey, their body language will be much more decisive, calmer, more controlled. Their pitch and tone will be even and exude confidence.

Decoding is simply the act of translating what was said by the sender into what it means to the receiver.

Static is the noise or other variables that interfere with the message.

Finally, feedback is quite important to both sender and receiver as it enables the sender to know for certain the information was understood correctly and allows the receiver to express their thoughts about the message.

The three main factors are:

- Words we use, or speech, makes up roughly 7% of face to face communication.

- Tone, which is the sound of our voice; the inflection, the pace, the enunciation and emphasis of words used, the modulation and pitch. These all give an indication of the sender's thoughts and feelings.

- Non-verbal cues, or body language, which includes several factors such as hand use, eye contact, posture, personal space and position, gestures, movements, non verbal sounds such as grunting, snorting, clearing one's throat, and much more.

Of these three, non-verbal communication includes tone and body cues which we will discuss further in the next chapter.

"Take advantage of every opportunity to practice your communication skills so that when important occasions arise, you will have the gift, the style, the sharpness, the clarity, and the emotions to affect other people." ~ Jim Rohn

Chapter 2 – What Did You Say?

Have you ever heard someone say, "listen to me, I know what I'm talking about!"?

It could be that their nonverbal message was different than their spoken one and they had to convince others or even themselves that they knew what they were talking about. Many people really don't understand the clues they give of their innermost thoughts and feelings or the mixed messages conveyed by their body language versus their spoken language.

Sometimes, we should be open and dare I say, even vulnerable; when we are expressing ourselves. Declaring your undying love and devotion to your partner is one such occurrence where openness is warranted, or maybe when we are engaged with our child or parent.

While there are some instances when being transparent is a good thing, however, those should be at your thoughtful discretion and not because you don't understand the social and verbal cues that you consistently use when speaking.

We all have "tells". That is, we all have mannerisms that we use when we are trying to hide something, when we are frustrated or angry or nervous, when we are being deceitful. Did you know that there are some expressions that are universally common?

Wherever you go on the globe, most people make the same expressions for fear, happiness, surprise, anger, sadness, and disgust. These can be overt gestures that are noticeable to anyone looking at them, or in the case of micro expressions, such small and quick gestures you have to be trained to see them.

Examples of emotions interpreted from facial expressions-- Tim Roth, lead actor in the TV show Lie to Me.

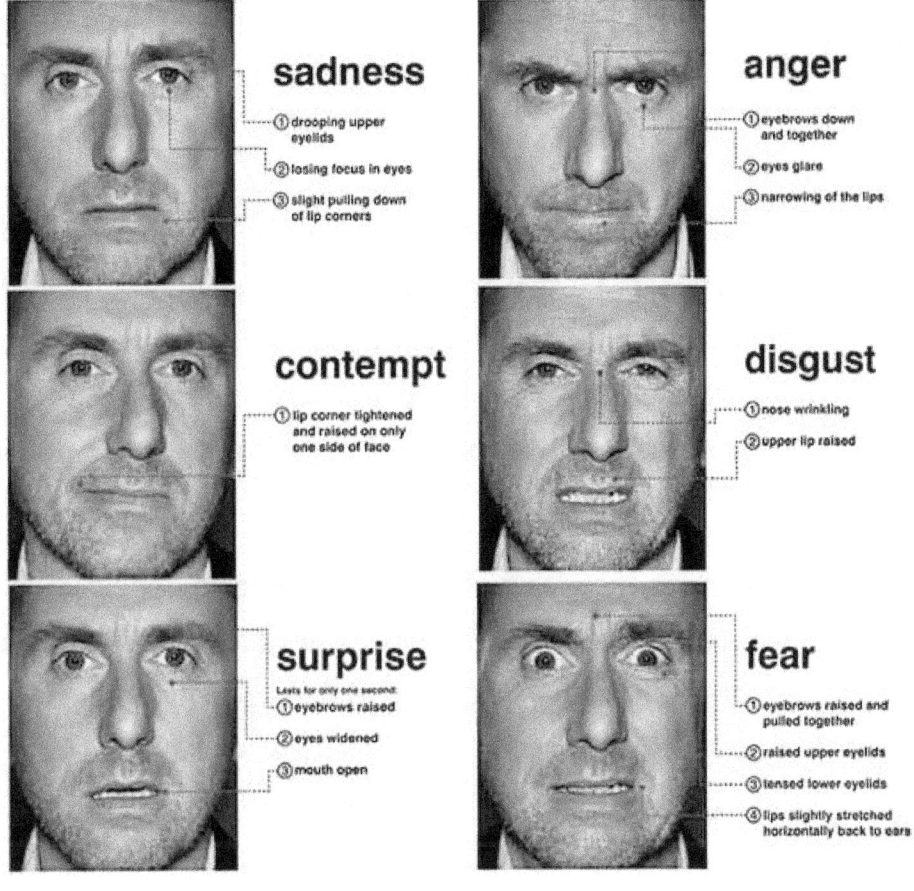

So how can you best present yourself in work situations, negotiations, when meeting someone new?

The first and best way to feel confident and well prepared is to practice, practice, and practice.

When you know that you will be giving a speech, you take the time to thoughtfully write your speech, practice it in front of a mirror, write the highlights on note cards, practice some more, and so on. You practice so much that by the time you get in front of your audience, you know your stuff and are comfortable saying what you need to.

You can prepare for a job interview or negotiation by studying the information needed or the topics of discussion you can anticipate, but what about those times when you are taken off guard completely; when your love interest calls at the last minute and says "oh, by the way, my mom and dad (whom you have never met) will be joining us for dinner."

Or you're at a night club and the most perfectly spoken and well dressed Mr. or Ms. Wonderful introduce themselves? At those times it is important to have an awareness of what your own body says to others and how to use body language to positively influence those around you, and possibly, yourself.

When meeting someone new, a firm handshake is the best introduction in most cultures. Be aware that cultural differences are an important thing to know though. In some countries it is frowned upon to touch someone at all and in others, it is offensive if you don't shake hands.

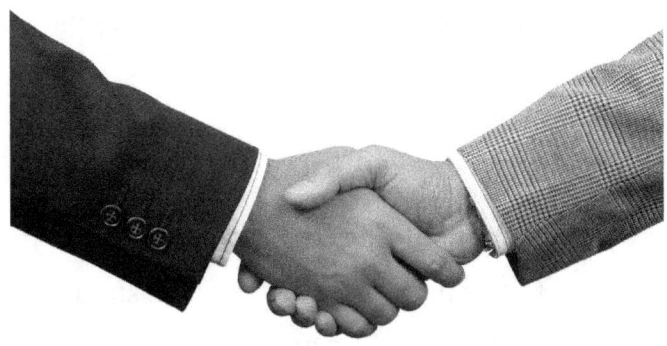

Different regions in the same country can have varying personal space exceptions, such as in the city or the country, and there are still places where it is taboo for a woman to shake hands with a man.

Know as much as you can about the culture you will visit or of the persons you will interact with so as to make the best impression.

According to author and speaker Allan Pease, we have more connections between our brain and hand than any other body part so the handshake is a very important indicator of a person's character, ideals, and interest.

"There are two key ingredients for creating rapport in a handshake. First, make sure that yours and the other person's

palms are in the vertical position so that no one is dominant or submissive. Second, apply the same pressure you receive. (2004)"

The vertical position maintains equality as neither of you are in the dominant (hand on top) position or the submissive (hand on bottom) position. Your grip should be secure but the pressure should be neither too light, which indicates weakness or surrender, nor too firm, which can indicate aggressiveness or dominance.

The fleshy part of your hand between your thumb and forefinger should be touching as well as the palm. Be aware that a limp, lifeless handshake suggests that the person is ill at ease or uncomfortable, while a double hand handshake, one where the palms are firmly clasped and one person's other hand covers the other person's hand reveal sincere feelings.

Another important physical cue is your hand and arm position. Most experts agree that crossing your arms is a defensive or closed body position and should be avoided as it gives the indication that you are "closed off" emotionally. Arms across the body with hands tucked under the elbows is the most closed position and indicates that you are not receptive nor open to ideas or information, or it can indicate submissiveness and fear.

Palm position is equally important. Open palms are a very positive cue fostering a sense of trust, confidence, and likeability. Conversely, a palm down gesture is more assertive. A palm down or pointing gesture is one of dominance, assertion, and power.

If you use your hands when you speak, and most experts advise that you should because it makes you more credible with listeners, if you want to foster a comradeship with your audience then keep your palms up but if you are emphatic and certain about your position and are choosing to take the role of leader then consider carefully how you use your hands when speaking.

While you want to look powerful, you might not want to look like you are domineering.

The way we interact with another when they are speaking can be very telling as well. If our facial expressions are impassive, this can be quite off-putting. A blank stare can indicate disinterest or even that you are not really listening but forming your reply while they are still talking. A half cocked or uneven smile can indicate deception, and covering ones mouth indicates that you don't feel it is safe or wise to say what you want to.

While we want to learn body language in order to "read" others, knowing what our own body is saying is quite valuable. Additionally, there are some ways that we can carry ourselves, and some poses, gestures, or stances we can take that actually help us to change not only other people's minds, but our own mind and emotions as well.

Amy Cuddy, a social psychologist, author, and speaker has spent years studying the effects of nonverbal behaviors. In her TED talk in 2012, she reveals that holding certain body positions or poses for two minutes can increase hormonal levels and change the way we see ourselves.

One such pose is called the "Wonder Woman" or the "Superman".

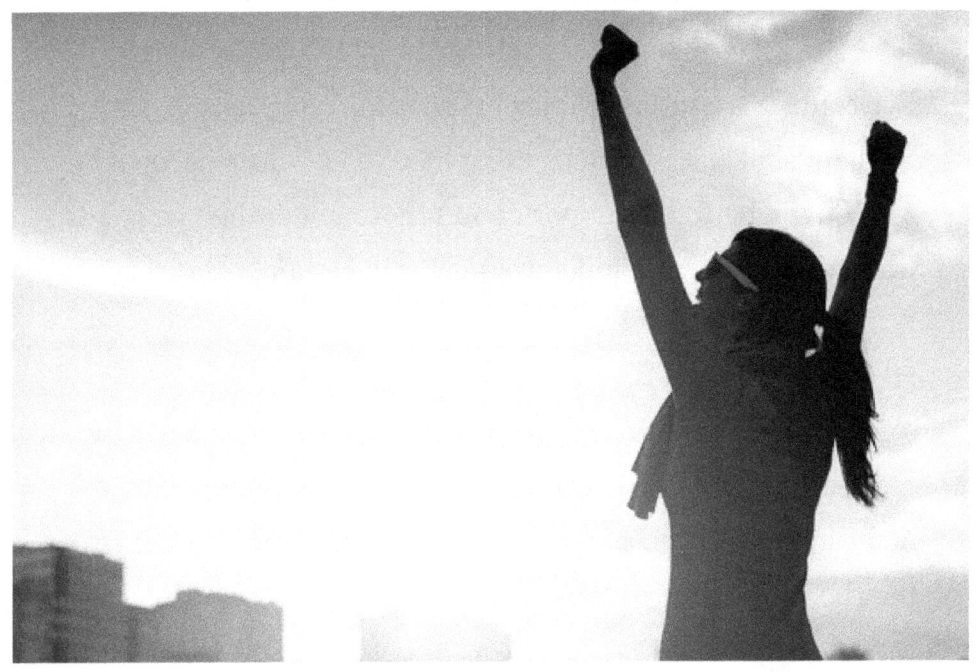

The hands are fisted and resting on each hip with elbows out, posture erect, and chin up. She proposes that standing this way, or in another powerful position for two minutes before a speech, an interview, a negotiation, or other such meeting can make you feel more confident and in control of your emotions.

What you do speaks so loud that I cannot hear what you say.

~ Ralph Waldo Emerson

Chapter 3 – Look Me in the Eye (or Don't)

Eye contact is another important body language aspect. Like the handshake, it is a tricky thing too. Some cultures frown on eye contact between a superior and those under their leadership, or a man and a woman, or in certain instances.

Again, know the culture of the person with whom you will be meeting when possible and give acceptable cues with your body language. It speaks volumes, especially when language may be a barrier or at least a hurdle.

Another important factor in eye contact is situational. In business, you don't want to give an impression of anger or intimidation, which is indicated by an intense stare directly in the other person's eye. The correct etiquette for eye contact when doing business with someone from the Western hemisphere is generally to look between the eyes and more towards the forehead.

More social eye contact is different and it actually takes practice to change your eye contact patterns. The key is to look intentional in business and natural in social situations.

When speaking with someone, a series of interested gazes rather than intent stares is appropriate, and when listening, be careful not to look away by turning your head as this indicates boredom or disinterest.

Blink rate is another important factor it seems. Blinking too much makes you appear dishonest or insincere, while not blinking at all can send a very similar message, or even a frightening one. The standard blink rate is 5-10 seconds between blinks.

While most people see averting one's gaze as an indication of deceit, discomfort, shame or embarrassment, there are other cues to consider before making a final character judgment.

Our eyes tell what we are feeling in other ways as well. Physiological tells that we cannot control are dilation or restriction of pupils. When a person is attracted to or interested in what they see, their pupils dilate. This is a natural body process that we have little to no control over.

As well as showing interest, "bigger eyes" are more attractive almost worldwide. Advertisers use this information as do toy makers. Take a look at most dolls, especially female dolls, and you will find oversized eyes. GI Joe and other action figures that are representing "strong, powerful men" have smaller, more intense looking eyes.

Where words are restrained, the eyes often talk a great deal.

~ Samuel Richardson

Chapter 4 – Head and Shoulders, Knees and Toes, and ...

So, maybe you're wondering what else comprises body language. What besides the hands and eyes give signals to those paying attention. Well, I'm glad you asked. So many things about us tell our story. Here are a few of those things.

Your posture is one thing that speaks volumes about you. If you enter a room standing erect, shoulders back and head at a slight upward tilt, you give an appearance of confidence, certainty, or power. People will notice you because you seem to "own the room" as you steadily walk through it.

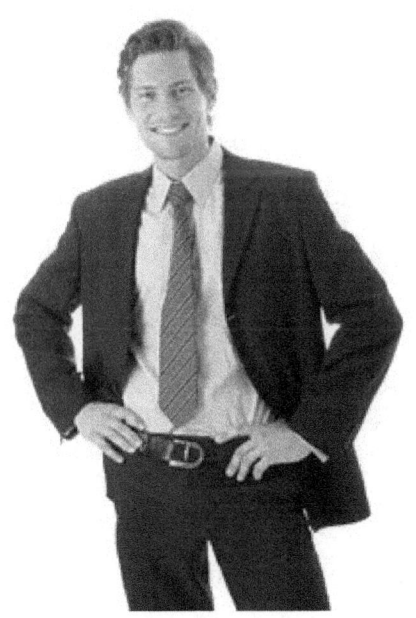

Quite the opposite is true if you enter that same room with slumped shoulders, a halting gate, hugging yourself or perhaps clasping your hands together tightly.

What you wear speaks loudly too. This may not seem fair to some because clothes can be expensive and we can't all go buy a new wardrobe every season, but simple clothing that is clean, wrinkle free, and in good repair, especially clothing appropriate to the event or situation is more favorably received than a dirty, or rumpled, or slovenly worn Gucci gown.

Any sort of adornment can be too loud if it is out of place or worn in a garish way. Wearing a pair of western boots with a frilly skirt is a fashion choice, but wearing a tight all black leather ensemble to your ex boyfriend's wedding, well that is a statement that can be heard by anyone within sight range. By and large, we stand out most in the best way when we aren't trying too hard to stand out from the crowd.

Another important social signal, whether in a business meeting or a mall restaurant is personal space. On average, about 18 inches is all we need between ourselves and those we have close relationships with, such as family, close friends, pets, or lovers.

For those we aren't quite as close to but still have more than a passing relationship with the amount of personal space needed is a bit more to the tune of 18 to 48 inches.

For those we only know socially, not that well at all really, the distance on average is over 4 feet but for the general public, given our preferences, we would stand over 10 feet away from the closest person. Of course, this is rarely possible in our modern world, at least in a city or a suburb. But, whenever possible, it is common etiquette to give a person as much space as they seem to need.

When someone's space is being "invaded" they might react by avoiding eye contact or avoiding any accidental touching by remaining unnaturally still. Someone's expression will likely stay blank when they are uncomfortable with the proximity of someone they don't know or are not intimate with and they will likely breathe more shallowly or slowly.

While some will remain expressionless and motionless, others might turn their back to the "intruder" as well as look away and close themselves off by covering their face with their hand or covering their chest with their arms or their bags.

Besides these, the tone of someone's voice can be an indicator of emotion more so than their words and the volume can be as well.

If the silent gestures we use with our body are a language, then the legs are their own dialect for sure. How we sit, stand, and walk are very telling informative about what we are thinking, how we feel, and what we intend.

For instance, standing erect, feet together and facing forward is called the "attention stance". It shows that a person is paying attention but has not decided one way or the other about the information they are receiving. Feet hip width apart and facing forward is a predominantly male stance that indicates masculinity, certainty, dominance.

You will find this used in groups of men where discipline and solidarity are the rule.

Legs crossed while standing is considered a defensive stance whether by a woman or a man. If a person that you are speaking with is standing and facing you with their legs crossed and their arms crossed, you have likely lost their interest in what you are saying or they have decided that you are wrong. These closed postures indicate that they have closed their mind to you and the ideas you are presenting.

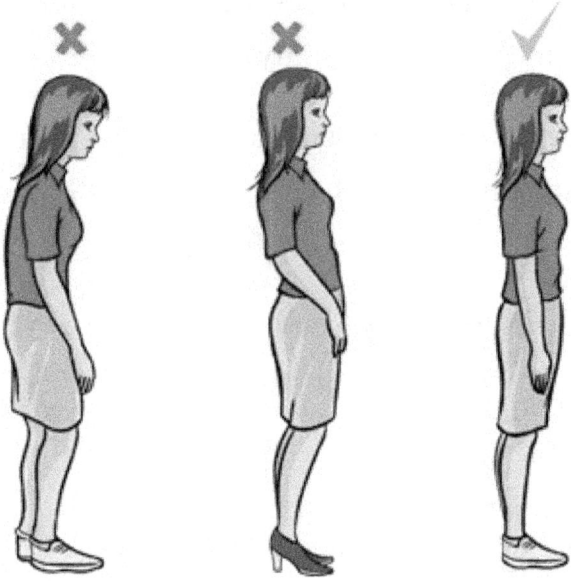

It is said that feet, being the furthest from the brain are the least filtered when they are speaking. If you are talking to someone who is in a seated position and their legs are crossed with the dominant foot pointed toward an exit, you might want to reconsider your tactic as they are ready to leave at the earliest possible point or at the very least, they have lost interest and have decided that the exit surely holds something of more interest to them.

A "foot-forward" standing position is a stance of certainty and decision. The dominant or "lead" foot points in the direction the mind most wants to go whether that is into the boardroom, or the bedroom. And think of this, when someone is not trustworthy, they are called "shifty".

Shifting your weight from foot to foot gives the appearance of dishonesty so next time you have a big proposal to give or a hot date, be sure to wear comfortable shoes.

It's true; the next time you have an opportunity to observe a group of people, check the feet. They lie far less than the lips.

He shifted his weight from foot to foot, but it was equally uncomfortable on each. ~Douglas Adams

Chapter 5 – Putting it All Together

If you mind is reeling from all the information shared so far, brace yourself. You see, this is an exceedingly wide topic. This is an important topic because communication is one of the most important parts of our lives. How we communicate impacts our relationships whether private, personal, or professional.

As with anything else, the impact can be positive or negative so knowing what your body is saying on your behalf is of the utmost importance. The value in this book is not in learning all you need to know about this subject, it is in learning that there is so much to know and that you can learn it over time by paying attention and putting in some effort.

 Imagine that you are a very shy person who has amazing ideas for inventions or songs or movies, or whatever. Now, imagine how hard it would be for a very timid person to get those great ideas across to the right patent attorney, the right musician, or the right producer if they could barely speak above a whisper when they were nervous.

If they finally did get a meeting with their target audience how would it look if they averted their eyes and crossed their arms over their body the whole time? Do you think they would be taken seriously? What is the possibility that they would win a powerful person in a position of influence over under those circumstances?

There is nothing wrong with any personality type, but if you have a timid personality, know the things that your body language are saying on your behalf and if that is not what you want to convey, you have the opportunity to learn better behaviors that do reflect what you do want to say.

What of the person who is the opposite? What if you were naturally loud, bordering on boisterous and the more nervous you became, the louder you seemed to get?

Being aware of how your volume affects others, you might try to tone it down a bit but those who are naturally boisterous tend to have "big" body language as well.

If you walk into a room and begin to grip and shake hands as if you were arm wrestling, you would naturally begin your event with mistrust and wariness as to your motives though you said very little at a modified decibel.

Every individual you meet has something to say. Whether they say it with their words or their body, knowing how to understand what they mean is an important talent that not many take the time to develop.

Polls reveal, not surprisingly, that poor communication is the number one reason for divorce. A whopping 65% of divorced couples list poor communication skills as the biggest factor in the dissolution of their family.

Listening is possibly the most important part of communication so understanding how to listen to the words and the body of a speaker is vitally important.

Here are some ideas for active listening and the body language that indicates this to others:

Active listening means that you are hearing not only the words that are spoken but you are picking up on the cues that give greater insight to what is meant as well.

When we are listening and we want to affirm what someone has said we nod our head. But be careful with nods as they are sometimes taken as agreement with rather than affirmation of a statement. It doesn't have to mean that we agree it is simply identifying that we heard what was said and if you couple the occasional nod with a phrase such as, "I hear what you are saying".

Our eyes are on the speaker and our face shows interest. Our lips may be relaxed or pursed depending on how we react to the information given, so be aware of the cues you are sending to the speaker as sometimes they are instinctive or habitual and happen with your even thinking about them.

The posture most indicative of interest is sitting straight and slightly forward, feet flat on the floor in front of us and pointed straight ahead, hands either at our side or possibly resting on a table or desk in front of us.

Be careful to focus on what is being said rather than preparing what you will say when they finish speaking, or being so focused on sending the right cues that you miss what they are telling you.

Like any other skill, active listening or being a purposeful participant in any form of communication takes practice but it is so worth it. Those with the ability to give positive body cues, to read the body language of those they interact with, who listen for understanding and try to understand what others are really saying, are by far the most successful people.

One last word of caution about becoming a student of body language; never use one cue to determine what a speaker means. There are several factors involved in each person's dynamic and all must be considered before making an important determination.

Factors that could possibly affect someone's body language might include a physical or mental disability or limitation, a person's culture or background, or even a current health crisis.

Be aware that you can be influenced by body language with or without your consent and you can influence others by your own body language whether you are aware of it or even whether or not you mean to.

Body language is a powerful tool. Understand it and that understanding thoughtfully.